Electronic Keyboard
Grade 4

Pieces & Technical Work
for Trinity College London exams

2015-2018

Published by:
Trinity College London
www.trinitycollege.com

Registered in England
Company no. 02683033
Charity no. 1014792

Marche Militaire

D 733 no. 1

Franz Schubert

arr. Andrew Smith

Voices: Brass, Clarinet, Flute
Style: March

PLEASE SET UP FOR THE NEXT PIECE

Dance Prelude

based on *Prelude in C minor* op. 28 no. 20

Frédéric Chopin
arr. Victoria Proudler

Voices: Choir *or* Pad, Synth Lead (e.g. Saw Lead)
Style: Dance *or* Trance

PLEASE SET UP FOR THE NEXT PIECE

Pizzicato

from *Sylvia*

Léo Delibes
arr. Joanna Clarke

Voices: Strings, Pizz Strings
Style: Hip Hop

PLEASE SET UP FOR THE NEXT PIECE

Santa Lucia

Traditional
arr. Rory Marsden

Voices: Classical Guitar (sounding octave lower), Mandolin, Strings
Style: Italian Waltz

PLEASE SET UP FOR THE NEXT PIECE

The Entertainer

Scott Joplin
arr. Victoria Proudler

Voices: Clarinet, Piano
Style: Ragtime

PLEASE SET UP FOR THE NEXT PIECE

7

I Do Like to be Beside the Seaside

John A Glover-Kind
arr. Nancy Litten

Voices: Honky Tonk Piano, Horns, Theatre Organ
Style: Theatre March *or* $\frac{6}{8}$ March

PLEASE SET UP FOR THE NEXT PIECE

Folk Song

Traditional
arr. Jeremy Ward

Voice:
Style:

* Candidates should refer to the current syllabus requirements for Own Interpretation pieces.

PLEASE SET UP FOR THE NEXT PIECE

High Wire

Andrew Smith

Voices: Brass Section, Clarinet, Piccolo (sounding octave higher)
Style: Tango

PLEASE SET UP FOR THE NEXT PIECE

Beautiful

Linda Perry
arr. Victoria Proudler

Voices: Alto Sax, Flute, Piano, Strings
Style: 8 Beat Ballad

PLEASE SET UP FOR THE NEXT PIECE

Separation

Nancy Litten

Voices: Guitar, Tenor Sax (both sounding octave lower), Strings
Style: Ballad

PLEASE SET UP FOR THE NEXT PIECE

Technical Work

Please refer to the current syllabus for details on all elements of the exam

i) Scales & chord knowledge

Ab major scale (two octaves)

E major scale (two octaves)

F minor scale: harmonic (two octaves)

F minor scale: melodic (two octaves)

F minor scale: natural (two octaves)

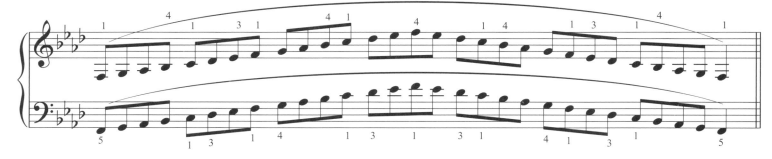

C# minor scale: harmonic (two octaves)

C# minor scale: melodic (two octaves)

C# minor scale: natural (two octaves)

A♭ major contrary motion scale (two octaves)

Chromatic scale in similar motion starting on A♭ (two octaves)

Chromatic scale in similar motion starting on E (two octaves)

Blues scale starting on C (two octaves), straight *and* swung rhythm

Right hand

Blues scale starting on G (two octaves), straight *and* swung rhythm

Right hand

A♭ major

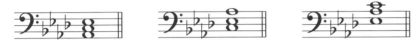

E major

F minor

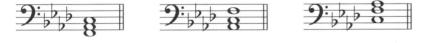

C♯ minor

A♭⁷

E⁷

Fm⁷

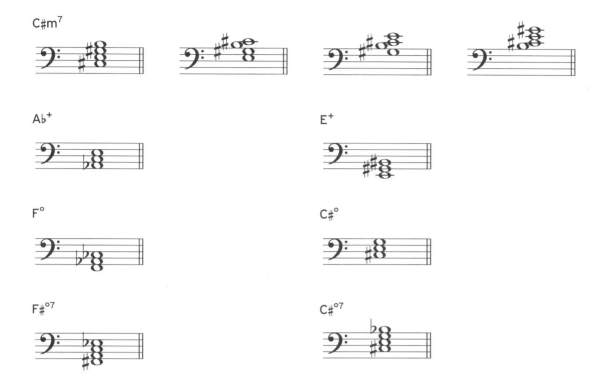

ii) Exercises

1. Deadly Nightshade – keyboard functions exercise

Voices: Electric Guitar (sounding octave lower), Sax
Style: Fusion or Pop Shuffle

please turn over

2. Hoedown – scalic exercise

Voice:	Violin
Style:	Hoedown

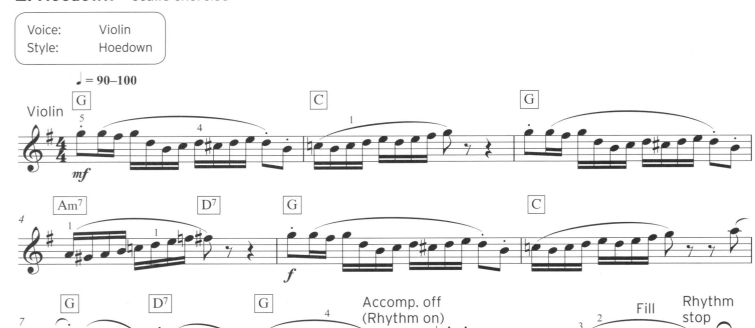

3. Old Times – pianistic exercise

Voice:	Piano *or* Honky Tonk Piano
Style:	None

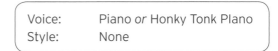